© Copyright 2024 David Merritt (Uncle Dave) All rights reserved. No part of this publication may be reproduced, distributed, or transmitted in any form or by any means, including photocopying, recording, or other electronic or mechanical methods, without the prior written permission of the author except in the case of brief quotations embodied in critical reviews and certain other noncommercial uses permitted by copyright law. For permission requests, contact dreamsinspiregreatness@gmail.com.

Special Thanks:
A special thanks goes to those who taught me how impactful words can be. I hope I can continue to use my words to be effective.

Wizards wonderfully wow us with words, with a wave and whoosh of their wands.

They say and speak such wonderous things, and what they say,

BECOMES.

We watch them display their magic in awe, wanting to be wizards too.

Well guess what? You're in luck. You can be a wizard also. Yes, it's true.

What kind of wizard can I be, you ask?
What can I create?

A Word Wizard? What is that? Never heard of such a thing.

Well lean in close and listen,
and I'll share with you everything.

Think carefully what you want to share. You're a Word Wizard beginner right now. We can help you prepare.

With the right words you can make someone

smile.

You can make them happy and

laugh.

You can make them feel good about themselves, even if they were before

sad.

You can greet people during your day with a, "Hi!" or "How do you do?" And they can reply, "I'm great! How about you?"

You can tell all kinds of stories. You can share the things you've seen and done. You can also share wonderful and wonderous tales, using your…

IMAGINATION!

Words help us **connect.**

There are so many ways to share.

There are dozens and dozens of different languages.

And there are many more

You can even be a Word Wizard with your hands.

Hello

Thank you

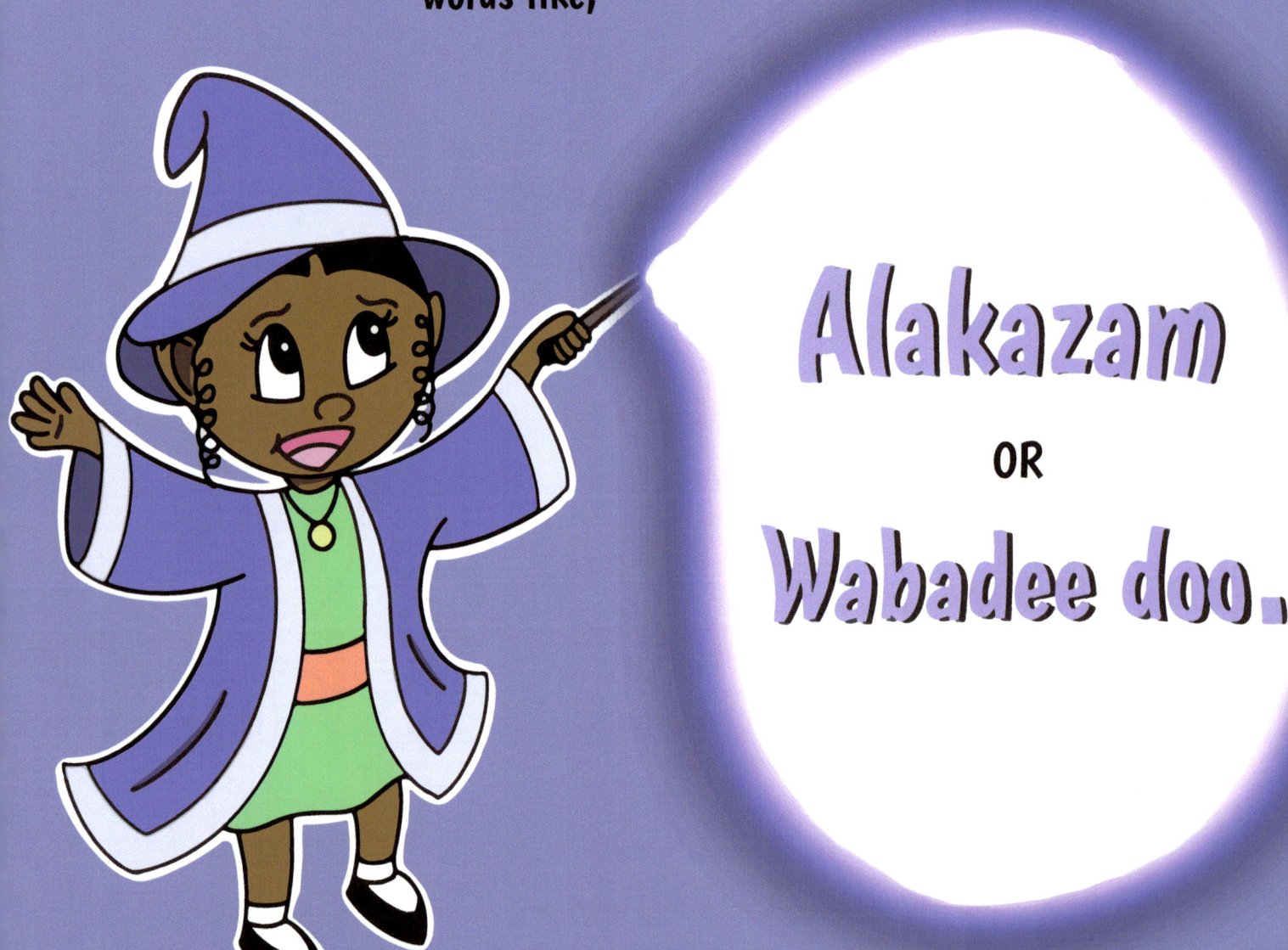

You can also use your words to encourage your friends, telling them, "I believe in you!"

Now be careful how you use your words.

So off you go my Word Wizarding friend.
Speak life and be full of glee.

What will be your story?

About the Author:

Thank you for coming along with me on this adventure. I've spent years reading about leadership and growing myself. After working with students for many years, I thought about being able to share leadership principles in a story format during a child's foundational years. It's my belief that when someone decides to build their dreams, what's most important in the beginning is building their foundation first. It's our foundations that our dreams are built and stand on. It's my hope that my books will be an effective tool and assist in laying down the foundation for people to grow and build their dreams. Thank you!

www.ingramcontent.com/pod-product-compliance
Lightning Source LLC
Chambersburg PA
CBHW060759090426
42736CB00002B/90